INSTANT SUCCESS

For Classroom Teachers, New and Substitute Teachers in Grades K through 8

by
Barbara Cawthorne

Illustrated by Jerry Paoli and Sylvia Prusakowski

Greenfield Publications
8720 East Forrest Drive
Scottsdale, Arizona 85257

For information contact:

Greenfield Publications
8720 East Forrest Drive
Scottsdale, Arizona 85257

With deepest gratitude to Bob Gray who made the creation of this book fun, and to my family for their support.

Library of Congress Catalog Card 81-82947
ISBN 0-9606666-0-5
Copyright© 1981 by Barbara Cawthorne
Second Printing, 1982
All rights reserved
Printed in the United States of America

ABOUT THE AUTHOR

Barbara Cawthorne graduated from Arizona State University with a degree in elementary education. Since then she has taught kindergarten through eighth grade and has worked as a homebound teacher. She has taught as a full-time teacher, but most of her teaching experience has been as a substitute teacher. She has also conducted seminars on substitute teaching.

Barbara finds that teaching full time is exhausting and does not provide absolute freedom after leaving the classroom at the end of the day. The advantages of full-time teaching are many; such as knowing your class intimately, working on specific learning needs, better pay, job security, and best of all, not being awakened at 6:30 a.m. for a teaching assignment.

However, Barbara finds substituting extremely rewarding after spending fifteen years in college and raising two boys. She now has the luxury of independence and scheduling work around her many interests. She states that when substituting, there are many ups and ego trips when the students see her and say, "Hurray, Mrs. Cawthorne is here today," or "I wish you were here for OUR class."

HOW TO USE THIS BOOK

The purpose of this book is to help a teacher feel comfortable when going into a new class by providing teacher-tested ideas and techniques. By dividing the book into well marked and easy-to-find units, the searching for material is simplified. Just go to the QUICK FIND GUIDE and thumb your way to the activity.

CODING:

Each page is coded by a symbol, upper grades (4 through 8) with a full symbol and lower grades (K through 3) with a half symbol.

 This half symbol means the activity on the page is primarily for children in lower grades, K through 3.

 This whole symbol means the activity on the page is designed primarily for children in upper grades, 4 through 8.

 If both symbols appear on the page, the activity is suitable for K through 8th grade children.

This is a general classification and may be used loosely. The ideas included are intended to spark the teacher's creativity. They have been proven in the classroom, but must be used with discretion. Those pages marked for copy master with a bar under the symbol are to be used by making heat masters (or making copies by whatever method is available) in the teacher's workroom.

Throughout the book the teacher is referred to as "she" and the student as "he." The purpose is for simplification in reading.

I encourage all readers to contact me if you have any questions or comments about any of the ideas included in this book, or if you would like your ideas to be included in any further printings with full acknowledgement. Please address all inquiries in care of Greenfield Publications. Good luck!

Barbara Cawthorne

QUICK FIND GUIDE

TABLE OF CONTENTS - 1

THE WARTY FROG

once upon a time

a warty frog

had a princess come along

and kiss it

        nothing happened

but when another frog

came up

        something did.

and for those of you

wondering what to do

while waiting

for your prince to come

I say

enjoy the frog.

Taken from SPEAKING POEMS, by Ric Masten, Sunflower Inc., Palo
Colorado Canyon, Carmel, California 93923.

INSTANT SUCCESS ©

Rapport Builders

This unit may be used to establish a good relationship with the students. It can also be used in conjunction with the Discipline unit.

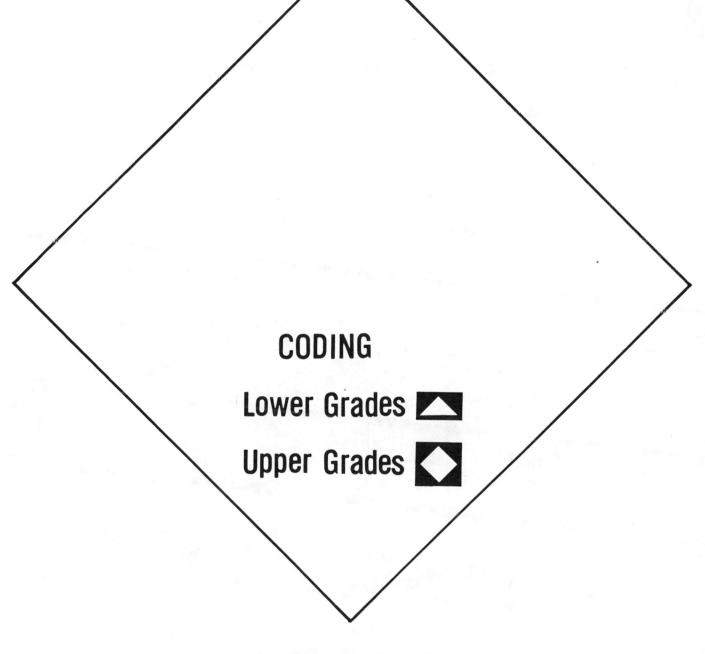

CODING

Lower Grades ▲

Upper Grades ◆

DOGGIE, DOGGIE YOUR BONE IS GONE

1. Choose one student to come to the front of the class to be the dog. He sits in a chair with his back to the class. An eraser (the bone) is placed under his chair.

2. The dog closes his eyes while a second student is chosen and takes the bone back to his seat.

3. The entire class puts their hands behind their backs and says together, "Doggie, doggie, your bone is gone."

4. The dog faces the class and has three chances to guess who has his bone.

5. If he guesses incorrectly, the student who took the bone gets to be the dog.

6. If he guesses correctly, he has another turn.

INSTANT SUCCESS ©

KING AND QUEEN

1. The teacher chooses a boy and a girl to stand next to their desks.

2. Each places an eraser on their head.

3. The teacher says, "King chases Queen." Then they walk quickly and carefully through the room as the boy tries to tag the girl.

4. If the Queen drops the eraser, the student sitting nearest to the Queen trades places with her and play continues.

5. If the King tags the Queen, the student sitting nearest to the Queen trades places with her and play continues.

6. Periodically, the teacher says, "Queen chases King" to reverse the play. The King and Queen then stop and the Queen now chases the King.

Note: If played with two boys, it is called King and Prince. If played with two girls, it is called Queen and Princess.

SIMON SAYS

1. All students stand up.

2. The teacher tells the students to do only the things Simon says. Then she says:

   "Simon says, 'Put your hands up.' (students put hands up)
   Simon says, 'Put your hands on your knees.'   (students put hands on knees)
   Put your hands on your head."   (teacher didn't say, "Simon says," so if any students put their hands on their head, they are to sit down)

3. Continue, going faster.

4. A fun way to play is to say: "Simon says, 'Put your hands on your toes,'" and the teacher touches her head. If any students touch their head, they are to sit down.

5. North-South directions and left-right discrimination may be used:

   "Simon says, 'Face North.'
   Simon says, 'Raise your left hand.'"

6. Play until one or several students remain standing.

INSTANT SUCCESS ©

FOLLOW THE STUDENT

1. The teacher picks one student to stand in front of the class to be the guesser.

2. The guesser turns around with his back to the class while the teacher picks another student to be the leader who remains sitting at his desk.

3. The guesser faces the class and the leader begins by clapping while the rest of the class copy his clapping.

4. The teacher says, "Change," and the leader then changes the activity and continues until five movements are given.

5. The guesser attempts to name the leader.

6. If correct, a new leader is chosen and the guesser continues.

7. If incorrect, the leader comes to the front of the class and becomes the guesser. The teacher picks a new leader and play begins again.

Other movements are clapping, raising right hand up and down, snapping fingers, clapping in back, tapping head, tapping stomach, and tapping desk.

SEVEN UP

1. The teacher chooses seven students who are sitting quietly to come to the front of the room.

2. One of the seven will be appointed caller. He begins by saying, "Heads down, thumbs up."

3. All students place their heads down on their desk with their eyes closed. Each student places a hand on the desk with the thumb extended up from a closed fist.

4. Each of the seven students must gently touch a student's thumb and quickly return to the front of the room. The person being touched places his thumb into his closed fist.

5. The caller then states, "Heads up, seven up," and the seven whose thumbs were touched stand up.

6. The caller asks each student standing to guess which of the seven students touched him.

7. Each student who guesses correctly trades places with the one who touched him.

8. Play is begun again.

Note: Game is best played for 8 minutes or less.

1. The teacher draws a scaffold, a stick man, and lines on the board showing the number of letters in a word.

2. The teacher chooses a student to guess a letter.

3. If correct, it is placed on the proper line or lines. If a word has duplicate letters, they are written at the same time.

4. If incorrect, the teacher draws the head of the man on the scaffold and the letter is written next to the scaffold so incorrect guesses are not repeated.

5. Students continue to be chosen to guess until the word or the man is completed.

6. No one may say the word until all the letters are written.

Note: May be used for reinforcement of spelling words.

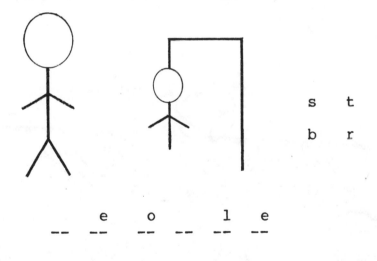

(correct word: people)

QUIET BALL

1. All students sit on top of their desks.

2. The teacher begins by throwing a large round ball to a student. The students then continue throwing it to one another. The ball is to be thrown gently and bad throws are the decision of the teacher.

3. If any student talks, has an intentional bad throw, throws the ball hard, hits windows or lights, gets off his desk, holds the ball for more than one minute, or misses the ball, he is out of the game and must sit in his chair.

4. The teacher is the judge and all decisions are final. If any arguments take place, a student is out of the game and must sit in his chair.

5. The teacher then continues the game by throwing the ball to another student.

6. The object is to see how many students can remain in the game.

What's worse than a giraffe with a sore throat? (a centipede with sore feet)

What's a caterpillar after it's three days old? (four days old)

If a papa bull eats a big bale of hay and a baby bull eats a small bale of hay, how much does a mama bull eat? (no mama bulls)

What's the best way to catch a squirrel? (climb a tree and act like a nut)

Why did the dying man need a dime? (to buy Life Savers)

What did one chimney say to the other? (you're too little to smoke)

What did one wall say to the other? (I'll meet you at the corner)

What time is it when the clock strikes thirteen? (time to get the clock fixed)

What do you do when an elephant hurts his toe? (call a toe truck)

Railroad crossing, look out for the cars. Can you spell it without any r's? (it)

If you put a mother duck and five ducklings in a box, what would you have? (a box of quackers)

How does a witch tell time? (with a witch watch)

What happens to ducks that fly upside down? (they quack up)

If you throw a white hat into the Red Sea, what does it become? (wet)

How many cubic inches of dirt are there in a hole one foot wide by one foot long by one foot deep? (none)

If a bull standing on three legs weighs 1000 pounds, how much will this bull weigh when standing on four legs? (1000 pounds)

What has four wheels and flies? (a garbage truck)

There were nine pigeons on the limb of a tree. A hunter shot three of them. How many remained? (none, the rest flew away)

It is advisable to use only a few jokes at a time exchanging a few with the students before starting assignments.

Gary: I've been seeing spots before my eyes.

Dave: Did you see a doctor?

Gary: No, just spots.

- - - - -

Fred: You know, Troy, the people upstairs are very annoying. Last night they stamped and banged on the floor until after midnight.

Troy: That's awful. Did they wake you up?

Fred: No, luckily I was up playing my tuba.

- - - - -

Crazy Cappy had two horses but he couldn't tell them apart. He tried cutting off the tail of one horse but that soon grew out again. Then he cut off the mane of the other horse. When that grew out again, he didn't know what to do. So he called up his Uncle Chuck and told him the problem. "Why don't you try measuring the two horses," suggested Uncle Chuck.

And that's how Crazy Cappy found out that the white horse was three inches taller than the black horse.

- - - - -

Aunt Rose: Why do you always snap your fingers?

Harold: To keep the tigers away.

Aunt Rose: There isn't a tiger within 100 miles of here.

Harold: It really works, doesn't it?

Sign in front of Mrs. Green's home: Anyone's welcome to use our lawnmower, provided he doesn't take it out of our yard.

- - - - -

Wendy: What is the best way to catch a fish?

Mark: Have someone throw it to you.

- - - - -

Dwayne: Doctor, will I be able to play the fiddle when my arm is out of this sling?

Dr. Cooper: Certainly, young man.

Dwayne: That's great! I have never been able to play a fiddle before.

- - - - -

Esther: Doctor, I get dizzy every time I look down.

Dr. Caplan: Then don't look down.

- - - - -

Kent Smith and his wife, Vicky, went to an air show. He was fascinated by the airplanes and finally asked a pilot how much a ride cost.

"Twenty dollars for ten minutes," the pilot said, "but I'll make a deal with you. If you and your wife can ride without making a sound, it'll cost nothing, but if you say one word, you will have to pay twenty dollars." "All right," said Kent.

They went for the ride and after the pilot landed, he said, "I want to congratulate you for not making a sound. You are a very courageous man.

"Maybe so," said Kent, "but I almost yelled when Vicky fell out."

Do they have a Fourth of July in England?   (yes)

Why can't a man living in Winston-Salem, North Carolina be buried west of the Mississippi River?   (he's alive)

Some months have 30 days, some have 31. How many have 28 days? (all)

A farmer had 17 sheep. All but 9 died, how many did he have left?   (9)

If you take two apples from three apples, how many do you have? (two)

I have been told that Moses took a certain number of animals of each species aboard the Ark with him. How many did he take? (none)

An archeologist claimed he found some gold coins dated 46 B.C. Why was he fired from his job?   (no B.C. on coins)

If a doctor gave you three pills and told you to take one every half hour, how long would they last you?   (1 hour)

If you had one match and entered a room in which there was a wood stove, an oil burner, and a kerosene lamp, which one would you light first?   (match)

It has been said that two is company and three is a crowd. What is four and five?   (nine)

If an airplane crashes on the border of Mexico and the United States, where would they bury the survivors?   (survivors would not be buried)

Two microbes are placed into a quart jar at 2:00 PM. They double every second. The jar is full at 3:00 PM. At what time was the jar half full?   (2:59:59)

If eggs cost 12 cents per dozen, how many eggs could you buy for $1.00?   (100)

If it takes three minutes to boil an egg, how long does it take to boil six eggs?   (three minutes)

Which is correct: 9 and 6 are 14 or 9 and 6 is 14?   (not 14)

GRAPHIC RIDDLES

1. The teacher writes a Graphic Riddle on the board.

2. The teacher asks those students who know the answer to raise their hands.

3. If several know the answer, they are called upon to help the rest of the class guess the answer by giving hints.

4. Only a few riddles should be used at a time.

1. sit ↓

2. stand
I

3. red
coat

4. time
time

5.
```
   R
   O
ROADS
   D
   S
```

6. wheel
wheel   drive
wheel
wheel

7. T
O
W
N

8. ground
feet
feet
feet
feet
feet
feet

9. noon good

10. person/ality

11. CCCCCCC

12. another one

13. head
heel heel

14. strokes
STROKES
s t r o k e s

15. cycle
cycle
cycle

16.
```
        J
YOU  U  ME
        S
        T
```

17. age beauty

18. gener ation

19. ecnalg

20. engage ment

21. if land
if if sea

22. gettingitall

23. eggs
easy

24. dice
dice

25. IDK

26. ttrroouubbllee

27. gseg

28. 000 circus

PRO FOOTBALL TEAMS

The teacher asks the students if they know the pro football teams. She then asks if anyone knows a football team with another name for the "King of Beasts."

Examples:

King of Beasts	(Lions)
747's	(Jets)
Indian Leaders	(Chiefs)
Rodeo Horses	(Broncos)
Rank of Boy Scouts	(Eagles)
Lubricators	(Oilers)
Hostile Attackers	(Raiders)
Seven Squared	(49'ers)
Make of Six Shooter	(Colts)
American Gauchos	(Cowboys)

INSTANT SUCCESS ©

1. Choose any number: 183

    Double it: 366

    Multiply the sum by 5:   1830

    Remove the 0:   183

    The answer will always be the chosen number.

2. Choose any number: 475

    Write the next four larger numbers: 476

                                                              477

                                                              478

                                                              479

    Add all five numbers: 2385

    Divide by 5:   477

    Subtract 2:   475

    The answer will always be the chosen number

3. Choose any number: 59

    Multiply by 3:   177

    Subtract 1:   176

    Subtract 1 again: 175

    Add the last three answers: 528

    Add the figures in the sum: 5 + 2 + 8 = 15

    If necessary add the figures.in the new
    sum until the answer contains only 1 digit: 1 + 5 = 6

    The answer will always be "6."

4. Choose any number: 634

   Multiply by 3:   1902

   Add 1:   1903

   Add 1 again: 1904

   Add the last three answers: 5709

   Add the figures in the sum: 5 + 7 + 0 + 9 = 21

   If necessary, add the figures in the new
   sum until the answer contains only 1 digit: 2 + 1 = 3

   The answer will always be "3."

5. Choose any number: 76

   Double it: 152

   Add 9:   161

   Subtract 3:   158

   Divide by 2:   79

   Subtract the original number: 3

   The answer will always be "3."

6. Write the numbers: 1 2 3 4 5 6 7 8 9

   Multiply by a favorite number: X   2
                                                   ----
                                                   2 4 6 9 1 3 5 7 8

   Multiply answer by 9:   X   9

   Answer is an interesting pattern: 2 2 2 2 2 2 2 0 2

Lesson Plans

This unit may be used "if" the teacher has not left any lesson plans, if alternate lesson plans are necessary, or to supplement existing lesson plans.

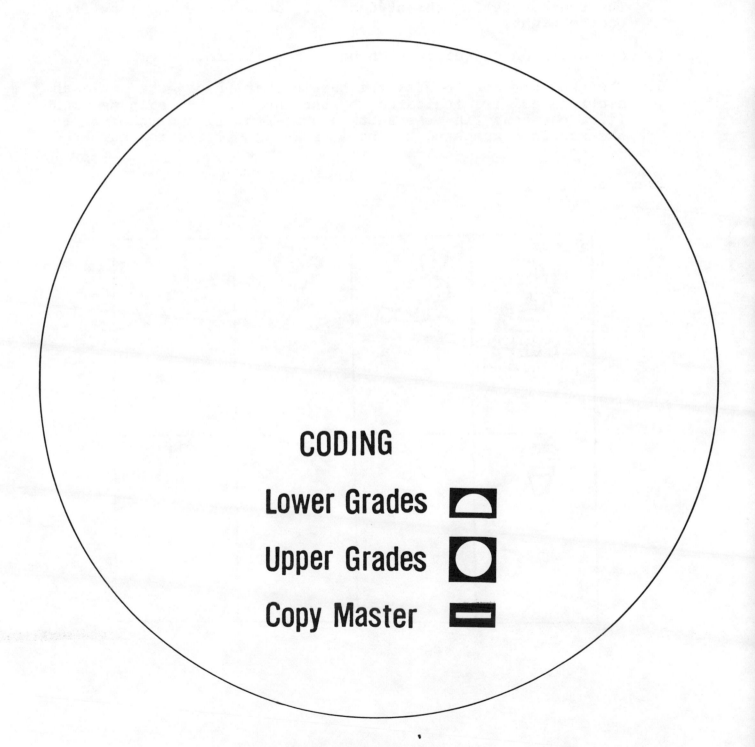

CODING

Lower Grades

Upper Grades

Copy Master

1. The teacher draws a rectangle on the board. The rectangle is divided into eight sections which are numbered sequentially from one to eight.

2. The students are given a large piece of paper which they fold three times to produce eight large sections.

3. The teacher tells the students to number the sections from one to eight.

4. She draws an object in each box on the board.

5. The students are to draw the same number of objects in each section as is indicated by the number in each section (i.e. one house in the section numbered 1, two rabbits in the section numbered 2, three trees in the section numbered 3, etc.).

Example:

INSTANT SUCCESS ©

WRITING SENTENCE OPPOSITES

Rewrite all sentences using the opposite of the word underlined.

1. I used some <u>black</u> paint.

   I used some white paint.
   ----

2. He went to the <u>back</u> door.

   ----

3. The road was <u>straight</u>.

   ----

4. My cup is <u>empty</u>.

   ----

5. The kite went <u>up</u>.

   ----

6. The clouds were <u>high</u>.

   ----

7. They said, "<u>Hello</u>."

   ----

8. The book is on the <u>bottom</u> shelf.

   ----

9. The parade went very <u>fast</u>.

   ----

10. My soup is <u>hot</u>.

----

11. Jackie is <u>asleep</u>.

----

12. The chair is <u>mine</u>.

----

13. I see an <u>old</u> man.

----

14. Here is a <u>little</u> spoon.

----

15. Jean gave the <u>wrong</u> answer.

----

16. The dogs are very <u>noisy</u>.

----

17. Ellen comes home in the <u>afternoon</u>.

----

18. Marge hurt her <u>right</u> foot.

----

19. Robin is a <u>small</u> baby.

----

1. The teacher cuts out five construction paper cats for the story (black, green, blue, yellow, and red).

2. The teacher reads the story on page 30 and holds up the appropriate colored cat at the beginning of each paragraph.

3. Scat the Cat is dittoed from page 32 and passed out to the students. The students color him their favorite color from the story. The students then cut out their cat.

4. The teacher retells the story. As a color of cat is described in the story, each student who has colored his cat the mentioned color is invited to bring his cat to the front of the room and hold it up.

5. The teacher may discuss the story with the students as to why Scat prefers to be black.

Once upon a time there was a little black cat and his name was
Scat the Cat. One day he looked around and saw that all his
brothers and sisters and all his friends were black, too. So he
thought he would like to be some other color. He said,

> "I'm Scat the Cat.
> I'm sassy and fat
> And I can change my color
> Just like that."

All of a sudden he was a green cat, green like the trees, green
like the leaves, and green like the grass. He went out to play
with his friends, and what do you think happened? His friends
couldn't see him because he was the same color as the grass and
the trees. So he didn't have anyone to play with, and he was
very unhappy, and he didn't think it was fun at all to be a
green cat. So he said,

> "I'm Scat the Cat.
> I'm sassy and fat
> And I can change my color
> Just like that."

And then what color was he? Yes, he was blue, blue like the
water, blue like the sky. He was so proud of his pretty new
color he decided to take a walk and let everyone admire him.
But do you know what happened? He came to a little pond of
water and he leaned way over to look at himself in the water,
and KERPLOP into the pond he went! Right down in the deep blue
water, and poor little Scat the Cat couldn't swim, and he was
so frightened he called for help. He called so loud that his
friends heard him, and they came to the pond. They looked down
into the blue water, but you know, they couldn't see him because
he was blue, just like the water. It just happened that his
friend, Timmothy Turtle, was swimming to shore, and he caught
Scat the Cat on his back and carried him safely out of the
water. Scat the Cat was very grateful, and he thanked his
friend over and over for saving his life. He decided he never
again wanted to take a chance like that again. He didn't
think it would be fun to be a blue cat any more. So he said,

> "I'm Scat the Cat.
> I'm sassy and fat
> And I can change my color
> Just like that."

And then what color was he? Yes, he was yellow, yellow like the
sun. He was very proud of his new color, and he decided he would
take a walk through the jungle. But who do you suppose he met
in the jungle? He met his cousin, Leo the Lion; and Leo said,
"What are you doing in that yellow coat? I'm the only animal in

this jungle that's supposed to be yellow!" And he growled so loud and so fierce that Scat the Cat was frightened, and he ran all the way home. He said,

"Im Scat the Cat.
I'm sassy and fat
And I can change my color
Just like that."

And then what color was he? Yes, he was red, red like an apple. He decided he would go out and play with all his brothers and sisters and all his nice friends. But what do you suppose happened? When his brothers and his sisters and his friends saw him, they all stopped playing and just stared at him. Then they started laughing and making fun of him. "Ha, ha, ha, whoever heard of a red cat," and no one wanted to play with him. They all ran away and left poor little Scat the Cat sitting there all by himself with no one to play with. He felt so sad. But he started thinking, and he decided he didn't want to be a red cat anymore because none of his friends would play with him. And he didn't want to be a yellow cat because only Leo the lion could be yellow. And he didn't want to be a blue cat any more because if he fell in the water, no one could find him to save him from drowning. And he didn't want to be a green cat because then he was just like the grass and the trees and none of his friends could see him. But you know, he decided he would rather be black just like all his brothers and sisters and his friends, and then he would have lots of other cats to play with. So after that, Scat the Cat was always happy being a black cat.

How many colors did he become?

                                        author unknown

1. The teacher reads the story on page 34.

2. Billy Goat Gruff is dittoed from page 35 and passed out to the students. The troll or the goat is colored by each student. If a student chooses the goat, he cuts the horns either short, medium, or long to designate Little, Big, or Great Billy Goat Gruff.

3. The teacher chooses four students with a different story character to come to the front of the class to pantomime the story with their character as the story is reread.

Once upon a time three billy goats lived by a hill. There was Great Billy Goat Gruff. There was Big Billy Goat Gruff. And there was Little Billy Goat Gruff.

The three goats liked to go up the hill to eat. The goats had to go over a bridge to go up the hill. And by the bridge lived a big fat troll!

One day Little Billy Goat Gruff started to go over the bridge. Trip, trap! went the bridge. "Who is on my bridge?" said the big fat troll in his great big voice. Little Billy Goat Gruff said, "Oh, it is I, Little Billy Goat Gruff. I must go over the bridge. I must go up the hill and get fat." "You can't go over my bridge. I will eat you!" said the big fat troll in his great big voice. Little Billy Goat Gruff said, "Oh please! Don't eat me. I'm too little. Eat Big Billy Goat Gruff. He is a big billy goat." "Get away from my bridge, then," said the big fat troll. Away the little billy goat ran. He ran up the hill to get fat.

Then Big Billy Goat Gruff started to go over the bridge. Trip, trap! Trip, trap! went the bridge. "Who is on my bridge?" said the big fat troll in his great big voice. Big Billy Goat Gruff said, "Oh, it is I, Big Billy Goat Gruff. I must go over the bridge. I must go up the hill and get fat." "You can't go over my bridge. I will eat you!" said the big fat troll in his great big voice. Big Billy Goat Gruff said, "Oh, please! Don't eat me. I'm too little. Eat Great Billy Goat Gruff. He is a great big billy goat." "Get away from my bridge then," said the big fat troll. Away the big billy goat ran. He ran up the hill to get fat.

Then Great Billy Goat Gruff started to go over the bridge. Trip, trap! Trip, trap! Trip, trap, trap! went the bridge. "Who is on my bridge?" said the big fat troll in his great big voice. Great Billy Goat Gruff said, "It is I, Great Billy Goat Gruff." He had a great big voice, too. "You can't go over my bridge. I will eat you!" said the big fat troll. "You will not eat me, I will knock you off this bridge," said Great Billy Goat Gruff. Then the big fat troll came up on the bridge. He ran at Great Billy Goat Gruff. Great Billy Goat Gruff ran at the big fat troll. Bump! Bump! Bump! Down went the big fat troll. Great Billy Goat Gruff knocked the big fat troll off the bridge. That was the end of the big fat troll.

Trip, trap! Trip, trap! Trip, trap, trap. Now the three billy goats go over the bridge every day. They go up the hill and get fat.

SNOWFLAKE

1. The teacher tells the students to cut out the circle on the solid line and fold on the dotted lines.

2. Fold the circle in half.

3. Fold the half into thirds on the dotted line.

4. Cut out small designs on the edges.

5. Open into a snowflake.

Example:

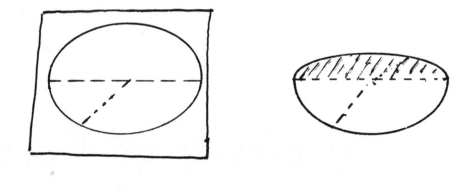

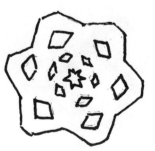

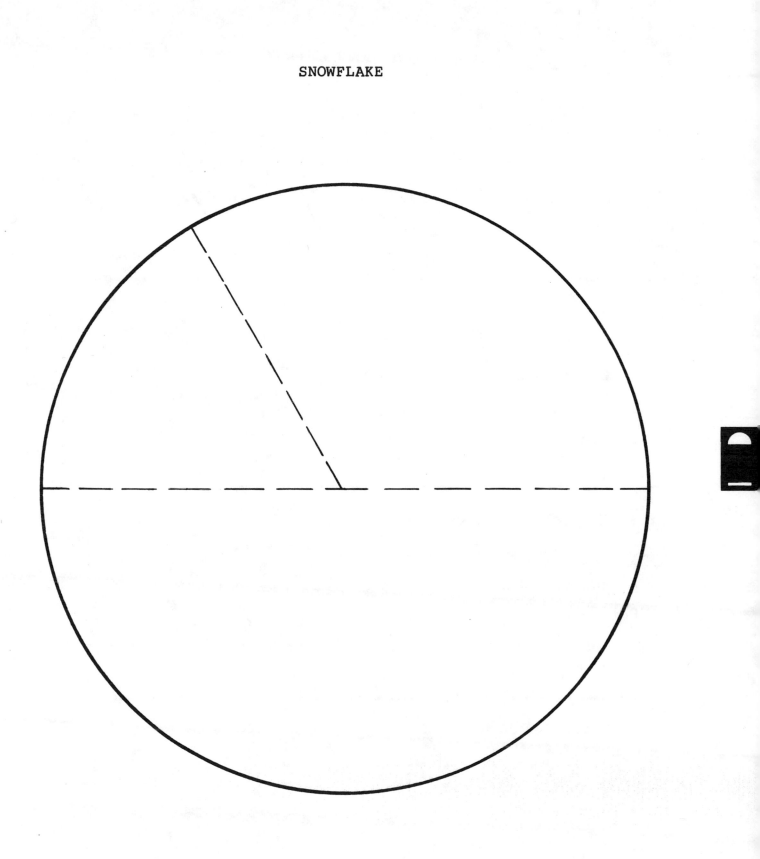

Color 7 diamonds green.

Color 1 diamond red.

Color the rest blue.

___diamonds are colored blue.

____ and ____ and ____ are 10.

Color 5 squares purple.

Color 3 squares yellow.

Color the rest blue.

___squares are colored blue.

____ and ____ and ____ are 10.

Color 6 triangles black.

Color 2 triangles white.

Color the rest blue.

___triangles are colored blue.

____ and ____ and ____ are 10.

Color 5 circles brown.

Color 4 circles orange.

Color the rest blue.

___circles are colored blue.

____ and ____ and ____ are 10.

INSTANT SUCCESS ©

MATH PUZZLE

Find the sums and differences. All answers equal to 7 are to be colored YELLOW. Color the rest BLUE.

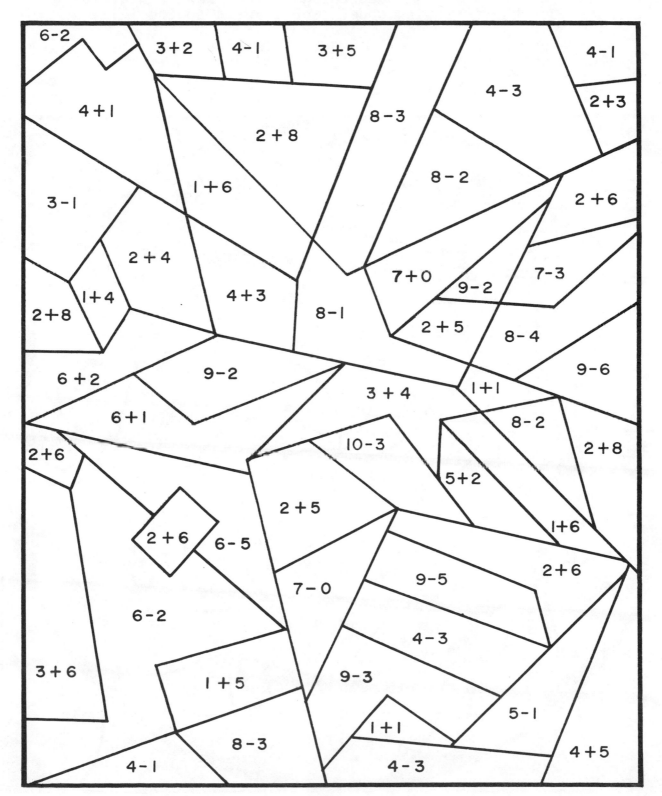

MATH DESIGN – Subtraction with regrouping

Work each of the number problems and write the answer by the problem. Color each area according to the last number in your answer. Use the following code. For answers ending in:

0 or 1 color RED
2 or 3 color BLUE
4 or 5 color BROWN

6 or 7 color GREEN
8 or 9 color YELLOW

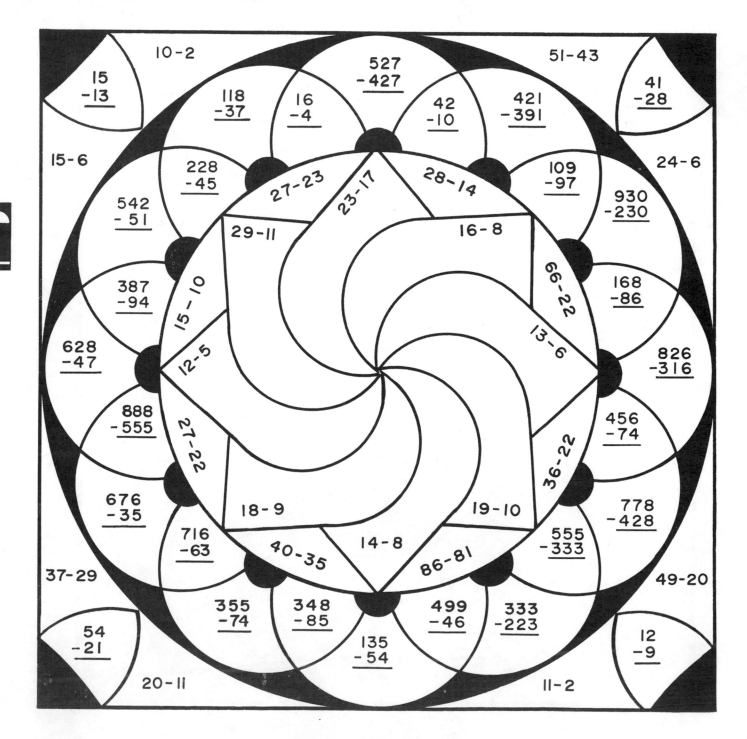

INSTANT SUCCESS ©

BINGO

1. Bingo sheets are dittoed from page 43 and passed out to the students.

2. The students are instructed to:

   Write a different letter of the alphabet in each square across the top line.
   Write a different one-digit number in each square across the second line.
   Write a different classmate's name in each square across the third line.
   Write the name of a different color in each square across the fourth line.

3. The teacher calls on the first student in a row and asks him to name a letter he wrote on the first line. The students who wrote the same letter place an "X" on that letter.

4. The teacher calls on the second student in the row and asks him to name a number he wrote on the second line. All the students who wrote the same number place an "X" on that number.

5. The teacher calls on the third person in the row and asks him to name a classmate he wrote on the third line. All the students who wrote the same name place an "X" on that name plus an "X" on the box marked FREE.

6. The teacher calls on the fourth person in the row and asks him to name a color he wrote on the fourth line. All the students who wrote the same color place an "X" on that color.

7. If anyone has four "X's" in a row, straight down only, "BINGO" is called. If no students have "BINGO," the game continues by starting again at step 3 with a fifth student.

8. When the first "BINGO" is called, play continues until at least ten students have called "BINGO."

9. The game may be played again by turning the paper over and tracing the Bingo design.

BINGO MATH

1. Bingo sheets are dittoed from page 43 and passed out to the students. The students write a math fact without its answer in each square. The math facts that are used (addition or subtraction) must have sums or differences no greater than twenty and no two math facts may have the same answer.

2. The teacher has twenty cards numbered 1 to 20. The teacher picks one card and reads the number. If the students have a math fact whose answer equals the number on the card, they place an "X" on the square.

3. When anyone has four "X's" in a row, down or across (including the FREE box), "BINGO" is called.

4. When the first "BINGO" is called, play continues until at least ten students have called "BINGO."

INSTANT SUCCESS ©

		BINGO Free	

MYSTERY MONSTERS

1. Each student is given a blank paper and asked to fold it three times into eight sections.

2. In each section a monster's part is drawn: head, right arm, left arm, right leg, left leg, shirt, pants or skirt, and hat.

3. Each of these parts are then cut out and glued together to make a mystery monster.

1. Each student is given a 6 X 9 piece of black construction paper and a 9 X 12 piece of white construction paper.

2. The white piece is folded in half.

3. A design is cut in the black paper.

4. Glue the piece of black paper on the front of the white paper.

5. Glue the cut out pieces of the black paper on the inside of the white paper.

6. The student will write his own special message inside the cover to his parents or someone special.

Example:

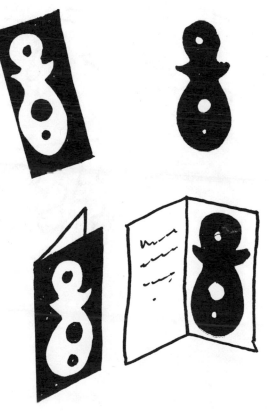

NAME ART

1. The students are given a piece of paper which they fold lengthwise.

2. Using a crayon, the students write their name along the edge of the fold and then trace over it so it is dark.

3. The paper is folded inside out. The back of the paper is rubbed to transfer the name to the other half of the paper.

4. The students darken the upside down name and then decorate the paper with color and design.

Example:

SPORTS GEOGRAPHY

Locate athletic teams on a United States map by placing the team numbers on appropriate states.

Baseball Teams	Football Teams
1. Baltimore Orioles	9. Atlanta Falcons
2. Boston Red Sox	10. Dallas Cowboys
3. Chicago Cubs	11. Denver Broncos
4. Cleveland Indians	12. Detroit Lions
5. Kansas City Royals	13. Miami Dolphins
6. Milwaukee Brewers	14. New Orleans Saints
7. New York Mets	15. Oakland Raiders
8. Seattle Mariners	16. Pittsburgh Steelers

SCRAMBLED EGGS

Unscramble the words to make names of birds or reptiles that are hatched from eggs.

1. niorb
2. rewn
3. cukd
4. skean
5. naws
6. rotsk
7. turyek
8. karpeate
9. yulejab
10. selugla

11. lagee
12. oirstch
13. sogeo
14. voed
15. leipcan
16. cniekch
17. tlutre
18. canyra
19. zirlad
20. galtilora

SPELLERS

Write the correct spelling for the following phonetically mis-spelled words. How many can you spell correctly?

1. ass-uh-9
2. lick-wuf-fi
3. phan-ta-sees
4. tra-key-oht-i-me
5. kon-shee-ehn-shus
6. im-pah-ster
7. mock-uh-sun
8. ah-kahm-uh-date

9. kon-sen-sus
10. hawl-lew-si-nayte
11. may-uh-nayze
12. in-ock-you-late
13. ren-eh-sans
14. fo-tog-rah-fee
15. re-sus-sah-tate
16. a-pro-pre-it

Our kon-sen-sus is that you need to in-ock-you-late your dog this afternoon in order to ah-kahm-uh-date the doctor. First, he is going to re-sus-sah-tate the a-pro-pre-it cat before it needs a tra-key-oht-i-me.

Mr. T

1. The teacher draws a "T" on the board.

2. The sample illustration below is drawn by the teacher.

3. Different types of Mr. and Mrs. T's are drawn on the board and potential stories are brainstormed with the class.

4. Paper is given to the students for them to draw their Mr. or Mrs. T.

5. A story about Mr. or Mrs. T is to be written on another paper.

Example:

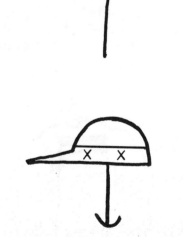 

INSTANT SUCCESS ©

CREATIVE WRITING

Story Starters

1. Each student is asked to pretend he is lost and finds him-
    self in a mysterious mist. As it passes, the student finds
    he is beginning to shrink smaller than a kitten. He is to
    write about all the problems he would have to encounter such
    as inside a house (lights, doors, furniture, food) and out-
    side a house (insects, friends, weather, cars).

2. The students are asked to pretend they are from another
    planet and have recently landed on Earth. The teacher
    brainstorms with the class and writes questions similar to
    the following on the board.

Examples:

What do you look like?
What was your home planet like?
What have you seen since landing on Earth?
How would you describe Earth's people (their appearance, food,
    recreation)?
Where are some special places you've visited on Earth?
What is it like living on your planet?

3. The students are asked to answer the following questions
    about their age.

Examples:

What are the advantages and disadvantages of being your age?
What's special about this age now?
What would you like to do as you get older?
What did you do that was fun when you were younger?
What is the best age to be and tell why?

4. The students are asked to write a mystery story using the
    following possibilities.

Examples:

Introduce characters and setting.
Discover a crime.
One person is the main character trying to discover the criminal
    and motive.
Keep introducing new things (secret door, another crime).
Narrow down the criminal, but don't let the reader know who it
    is.
Solve the crime including how and why it was committed.
Capture the criminal.

The House

1. The picture on page 54 can motivate students to create moods, interpret the setting through visual clues, and form sensory images.

2. The students answer the ditto questions on page 53.

3. The students write a story based on the ditto questions and the picture of the house.

4. The students color the house to reflect the mood they wish.

5. Run question and house dittos back to back to conserve paper.

INSTANT SUCCESS ©

THE HOUSE

First look at the house, then answer the following questions:

1. What season of the year is it (trees, grass, sky)?

    ----

2. What are some details about the house (age, number of rooms, decor in the house, basement, attic, play room, other rooms)?

    ----

3. Where is the house located (country, lonely road, downtown)?

    ----

4. What is special about this house (cheerful, gloomy, size)?

    ----

5. Why would (wouldn't) you live in this house?

    ----

6. Does it look like anyone is living in this house? Why?

    ----

7. Who would live in this house (you, no one, elderly people, a large family, college students, ghosts, rich or poor people)? Why?

    ----

8. Write a story on another piece of paper about your experiences after spending a few days in the house.

CREATIVE WRITING

Who Am I?

1. Each student is asked to write a description of himself. He is to tell where and when he was born, his sex, color of hair, color of eyes, interests, his family, favorite TV programs and movies, special friends, etc.

2. The teacher reads each student's descriptive paper without reading the student's name.

3. The teacher calls on students to guess who the student is.

CREATIVE WRITING

Personification Ideas

1. The teacher tells the students to pretend for one entire day that they may become any object in the world.

2. She asks them, "What would it feel like? What unusual things might happen to you?"

3. The students are asked to write a story about their day. When the story is finished, they are to draw a picture of the object they have become.

4. A few of the following are suggested to the students (they may think of others).

Examples:

the pencil of a student taking a test
a doorbell on Halloween
the principal's desk
the shoe of a famous football player
the last two cookies in the cookie jar
a Christmas stocking talking to Santa Claus
a lawn of tall grass talking to a lawnmower
two goldfish being observed by a class
a desk and chair of a boy who is absent from school
the last two chocolates in a box of candy
two crayons in a student's desk
the only two empty swings on the school playground
a towel talking to a wash cloth seldom used by a small boy
a new brand of toothpaste talking to some teeth
one owl to another while some Cub scouts are "bravely" camping
    out for the first time

Example of a story:

"The Day I Became a Pencil"

I was clutched tightly in the grip of a student. It was that time of year again. This was math class. How I disliked this! I felt dampness all over my skinny body, because my owner's hand perspired as if he were scared. Oh, no! He's getting nervous and is starting to chew on me. Ouch! How that hurts!

INSTANT SUCCESS ©

CREATIVE WRITING

It's Going to Be a Bad Day when ...

1. Ask the students if they have ever had a bad day. Allow several students to share their experiences with the class.

2. The students are to write a story using their own ideas or completing one of the following humorous possibilities for a bad day.

Examples:

You turn on the news and they are showing emergency routes out of the city.
Your twin sister forgot your birthday.
Your car horn goes off and sticks as you follow a policeman on the freeway.
The bird singing outside your window is a buzzard.
You wake up and your braces are hooked together.
You put both your contact lenses in the same eye.

What Would Happen if ...

1. Ask the students if they have ever dreamed of supernatural situations. Allow several students to share their experiences with the class.

2. The students are to write a story using their own ideas or completing one of the following possibilities.

Examples:

Man could fly without aids.
A hole was bored through the center of the earth.
Man could live forever.

GUESS WHO

1. The name of an animal or person is taped on the backs of the students without them knowing what name is taped on their backs.

2. The students walk around the room asking questions which are answered only by yes or no. Students may act out the character on the other students' backs.

3. The objective is for the students to successfully identify the animals or people who are taped on their backs.

4. As each student thinks he knows who he is, he is to sit down. There is approximately a 15 minute time limit for this activity.

5. At the end of the time limit, the teacher goes to each student and asks him who he is and removes the name on his back. After the student responds (either with a guess or an "I don't know"), the teacher shows the name to the student and class.

Examples of animals:

alligator, bear, bird, camel, cat, cow, deer, dog, duck, elephant, fox, frog, giraffe, goat, hamster, horse, lion, lizard, monkey, mouse, pig, rabbit, raccoon, sheep, snake, seal, tiger, turtle, zebra

Examples of people:

Christopher Columbus, George Washington, Thomas Jefferson, Abraham Lincoln, John Kennedy, Richard Nixon, Winston Churchill, General George Patton, Madam Curie, Eleanor Roosevelt, Thomas Edison, Henry Ford, Albert Einstein, George Washington Carver, Martin Luther King, Robert E. Lee, Napoleon, Groucho Marx, Elvis Presley, Robert Redford, Bob Hope, Jack Benny, George Burns, Marilyn Monroe, Wonder Woman, Superman, Spiderman, Geronimo, William Shakespeare, Mark Twain, Lenin

INSTANT SUCCESS ©

STIMULATORS FOR READING TEXT BOOKS

The teacher may use the following to stimulate interest in reading assigned textbook pages.

1. The class may do the assignment together, in small groups, or individually.

2. The class may write a test. Each student writes one question with the answer on the back of his paper. The teacher collects the questions and asks the class to answer them orally.

3. The teacher reads an important concept from assigned text book pages. Then she calls on a student to read the next sentence.

4. A debate is simulated between characters in a history assignment.

5. The students prepare a short report about the assigned subject. When finished, they lecture to the class when called upon by the teacher.

6. The teacher asks the class to think of five ideas that they think will be covered in a reading assignment before they start reading. Each student is to write his five ideas on paper and check the accuracy of his guesses as he reads.

Math

1. The teacher divides the class into two teams with an equal number of students on each team.

2. If there are thirty students in the class, the members of each team are assigned a number from 1 to 15. (If there are thirty-one students in the class, one team member is assigned two numbers.)

3. An identical math problem is written on the board in two different places.

4. The teacher calls out a number from 1 to 15.

5. The pair of students with that number (one from each team) walk quickly to the board and work their problem. Each team member who works the problem correctly wins a point. The other students may work the problem at their desks and verify the answer.

History (played the same way except the teacher asks historical questions)

Examples:

What year was the Declaration of Independence signed?
How many colonies signed the Declaration of Independence?

Geography (played the same way)

Examples:

Name a state beginning with an "O" and locate it on the map.
What is the capital of Maine?

Spelling (played the same way, but the teacher asks spelling words)

T RELAY

1. The teacher divides the class into two teams with an equal number of students on each team.

2. The teacher has one member from each team come to the board.

3. The players each draw a large "T" on the board.

4. The teacher calls off five numbers which are written on the left side of the "T."

5. The teacher then calls, "Times 3," (or plus 6, minus 4, etc.) which the players write at the top of the "T" before solving the problems.

6. Each student who works the problems accurately earns a point for his team.

7. Students at their desks will also work the problems to verify if team members are correct.

Example:

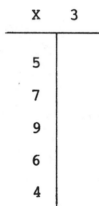

CROSSWORD MATH

Solve by Multiplication.

Across

a. 41 X 9

c. 55 X 4

e. 15 X 15

g. 21 X 7

i.   9 X 5

j.   6 X 8

k. 53 X 8

m. 35 X 10

n.   7 X 49

p. 28 X 4

Down

a. 14 X 28

b. 48 X 20

d.   3 X 9

e. 14 X 16

f. 17 X 32

g. 61 X 3

h. 30 X 25

l. 16 X 4

n. 43 X 7

0.   8 X 39

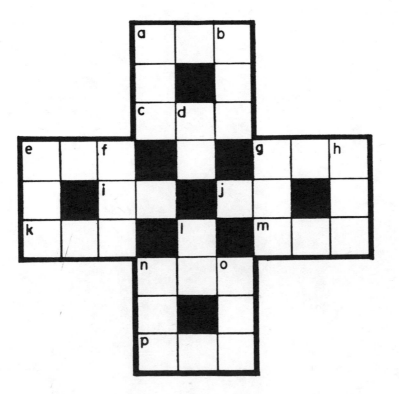

INSTANT SUCCESS ©

CROSSWORD MATH

Solve by Adding, Subtracting, Multiplying, or Dividing.

Across

a. 2592 ÷ 6
c. 3 X 153
e. 36 + 28
f. 2646 ÷ 42
j. 3 X 210
m. 2 X 342
n. 4393 - 1425
o. 1798 + 1754
p. 79 X 8
r. 17 + 13
s. 532 + 429
u. 189 - 175
x. 122 - 43
A. 171 X 4
B. 111 + 73

Down

b. 1205 ÷ 5
c. 3376 - 2914
d. 4 X 39
g. 857 - 593
h. 292 ÷ 4
i. 45 + 53
k. 24765 ÷ 5
l. 5 X 930
p. 3 X 204
q. 16 + 18
t. 4416 ÷ 23
v. 432 + 432
w. 7 X 53
y. 49 X 2
z. 134 - 96

MAGIC SQUARE MATH

No matter which column of numbers is added, the answer is always the same (down, across, or diagonally).

Example:

4	6	2
2	4	6
6	2	4

(all columns add up to 12)

Solve:

3	4	2

(make all columns add up to 9)

Multiply columns across and down for the magic number in the box.

Example:

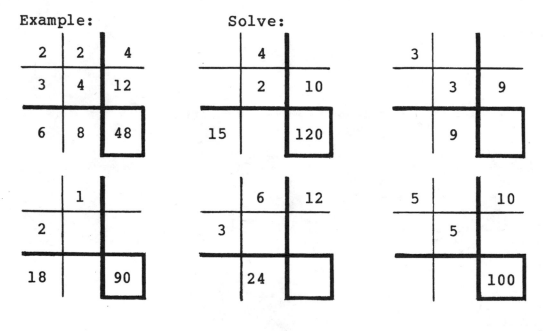

Solve:

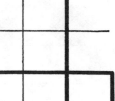

Make Your Own:

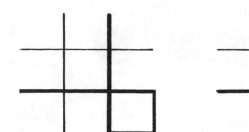

INSTANT SUCCESS ©

Spare Time Assignments

This unit may be used for any student who completes all teacher directed assignments. Most of the pages within this unit are self-explanatory.

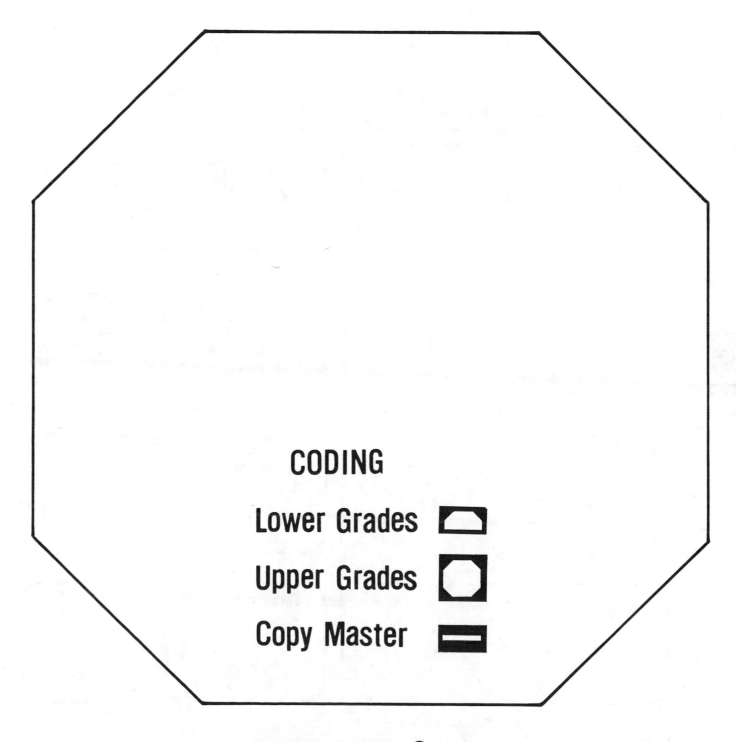

CODING

Lower Grades

Upper Grades

Copy Master

Put the animals in ABC order with the one that comes first in the box with a 1.

elephant **seal**
zebra **bear**
monkey **lion**
alligator **tiger**

INSTANT SUCCESS ©

CUT AND GLUE OPPOSITES

Find the opposite of the first word and put it in the box with a 1.

1. above   4. open   7. asleep

2. first   5. empty   8. begin

3. under   6. black

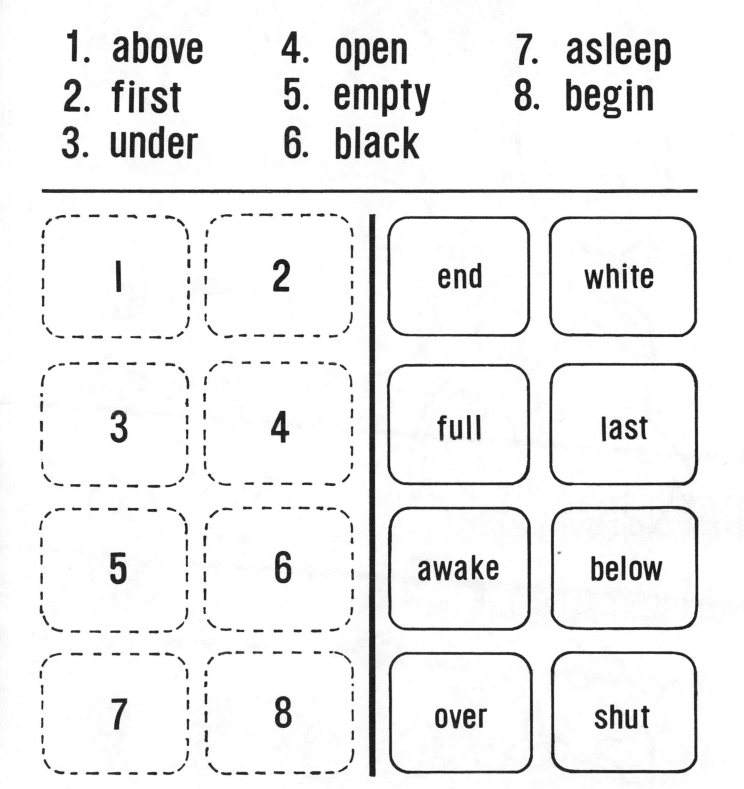

1	2	end	white
3	4	full	last
5	6	awake	below
7	8	over	shut

INSTANT SUCCESS ©

SHOE ART

Trace your shoe on a piece of paper and create a picture.

Add some lines to create a picture.

INSTANT SUCCESS ©

How many different things can you make from a circle?

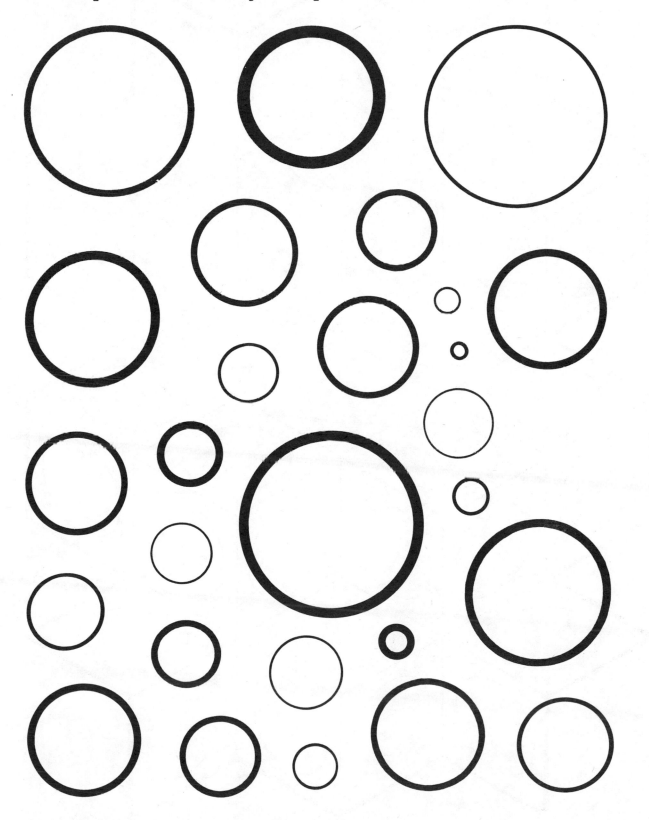

INSTANT SUCCESS ©

SCRAMBLED MONTHS

The words below are the names of the months or periods of time (day, week, month, year) that have been scrambled. Unscramble the letters to find the name of the month or period of time. Put the correctly spelled words in the puzzle.

Across

1. HOMTSN
6. RLIPA
8. BMCEREDE
12. TUGASU
13. BUYFERAR
14. RAEY
15. KEWE

Down

1. YAM
2. PESTBMERE
3. RACMH
4. LUYJ
5. UNJARAY
7. BOCTEOR
9. REBNOVME

10. YDA
11. JENU

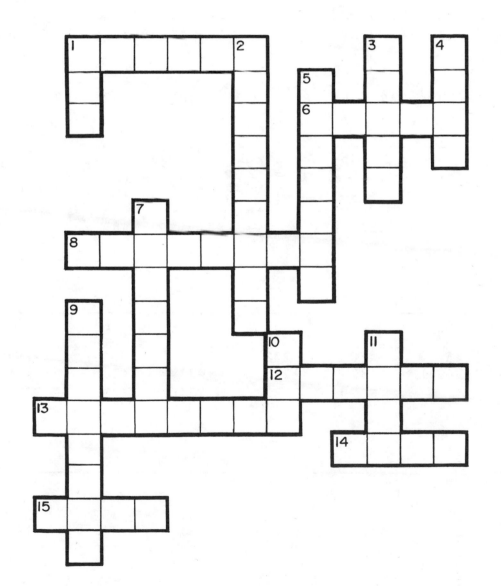

DECODE THE RIDDLE - Addition with no regrouping

Work the math problems. Then decode the riddle by putting the correct letters in the blanks above the numbers.

```
 ---   ---   ---   ---        ---   ---   ---   ---   ---   ---
 695   477   887   992        887   342   695   887   679   299

 ---   ---   ---   ---   ---   ---   ---         ---         ---   ---   ---   ---
 582   666   342   342   666   695   299         887         342   552   666   894
                                                                                  ?
 ---   ---   ---   ---   ---   ---   ---   ---   ---   ---
 599   972   599   281   679   695   477   599   281   599

             ---   ---   ---        ---   ---   ---   ---
             477   552   299        992   887   552   342
```

A	E	F	H	I	L	N
463	257	450	242	121	242	791
+424	+342	+132	+235	+431	+100	+103
----	----	----	----	----	----	----

O	R	S	T	V	W	Y
333	150	135	271	641	352	530
+333	+131	+164	+721	+331	+343	+149
----	----	----	----	----	----	----

INSTANT SUCCESS ©

DECODE THE RIDDLE - Subtraction with regrouping

Work the math problems. Then decode the riddle by putting the correct letters in the blanks above the numbers.

---	---	---	---		---	---	---	---		---	---	---
338	256	588	47		256	588	485	485		77	274	82

---	---		---	---	---		---	---	---		---	---		---
588	47		47	256	77		77	274	483		557	68		588

?

---	---	---		---	---	---	---	---		---	---	---	---
483	165	386		82	485	77	389	389		165	588	379	274

A	D	E	F	H
985 -397 ----	621 -138 ----	374 -297 ----	815 -747 ----	643 -387 ----

I	L	N	O	P
715 -336 ----	831 -442 ----	432 -158 ----	915 -358 ----	614 -129 ----

R	S	T	W	Y
443 -278 ----	541 -459 ----	232 -185 ----	832 -494 ----	584 -198 ----

ANIMAL WORD SEARCH

Circle the names of the animals which can be found within this
word search. The names are written across, down, and diagonally.

```
h  c  a  f  r  c  a  t  o  p
d  o  g  r  o  w  e  i  b  e
i  w  r  o  m  x  b  g  z  d
p  i  g  s  t  d  i  e  m  e
u  t  o  w  e  u  r  r  s  e
b  v  a  n  d  c  d  w  e  r
z  e  t  g  y  k  e  y  a  k
s  g  a  j  a  c  t  z  l  n
s  t  a  r  s  p  f  i  s  h
r  u  n  t  o  n  e  t  w  o
```

Animal names found in word search:

ape	cat	dog	fox	pig
bear	cow	duck	goat	seal
bird	deer	fish	horse	tiger

INSTANT SUCCESS ©

SEASONAL SPORTS ACTIVITIES

Unscramble the words that name seasonal sports activities.

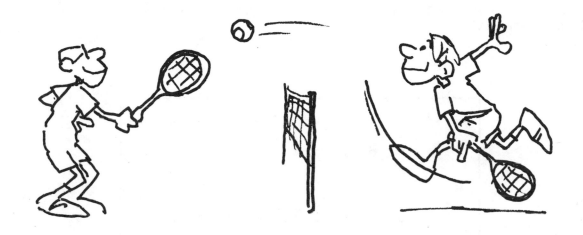

FALL	TOFOLABL	KSACJ
	HOTPSOCHC	CERCOS
	MUPJ REOP	SELBRAM
WINTER	HEYOCK	BELASTBAKL
	KINGSI	NASTICSGYM
	INGDDELS	CIE TIKAGNS
SPRING	NITSEN	CATRK
	SEKIT	SABLABEL
	GINHIK	CLIGNBICY
SUMMER	PANCIMG	BAOTNIG
	SHINIFG	SUFGINR
	FOLG	MIGSINWM

PAST TENSE WORD SEARCH

Many verbs add "ed" to form the past tense although not all verbs add "ed". Some verbs change their spelling completely, so break becomes broke when the action occurred in the past. Change the 15 verbs listed below to their past tense form. Then circle them in the puzzle. They are written across, down, and diagonally.

```
w  e  n  f  s  c  a  u  g  h  t  l
t  o  f  d  p  a  i  d  i  d  i  g
b  e  r  l  r  w  l  t  m  h  d  r
r  w  o  e  y  a  l  o  d  s  f  e
o  d  z  g  p  u  n  o  m  r  o  w
u  t  e  n  s  w  e  k  s  w  u  l
g  e  r  r  p  z  a  l  r  t  g  h
h  t  f  r  o  e  n  l  e  e  h  e
t  o  i  d  k  s  l  e  f  t  t  a
a  r  f  l  e  e  e  a  e  l  s  r
n  a  o  s  h  o  o  k  r  e  e  d
m  d  g  t  a  r  o  s  e  l  e  w
```

1. arise _____   6. fly _____   11. lose _____

2. bring _____   7. freeze _____   12. pay _____

3. catch _____   8. grow _____   13. shake _____

4. drink _____   9. hear _____   14. take _____

5. fight _____   10. leave _____   15. wear _____

INSTANT SUCCESS ©

CLOTHING WORD SEARCH

Circle the names of the clothing which can be found within this word search. The names are written across down, and diagonally.

```
t a b l b l o u s e d o l l y j
c r a f g g r a n k t r o b e t
s t a n d l p s o a i p e v t o
c o l l a r o a s h o r t s h w
l o h b c s w v j h i m t n s e
s c a r f m l j e a i u g o w n
w b n t d q u i v s m r y o t e
l e d c o a t f c e b a t s p r
m l k s u i t p u o t e s l i p
i t e f n e v x f b s o l a j c
t x r g o t i e f u z d i c a p
t s c h m b t a s t i p p k c r
e r h t h f o r a t p a p s k o
n z i m a y m o r o p n e f e a
s w e a t e r l t n e t r c t d
v m f k p s o c k s r s h o e s
```

Clothing names found in word search:

belt	gown	robe	slip
blouse	handkerchief	scarf	slipper
boots	hat	shirt	socks
cap	jacket	shoes	suit
coat	mittens	shorts	sweater
dress	pajamas	skirt	tie
gloves	pants	slacks	vest

UNITED STATES WORD SEARCH

Circle the names of the 50 states which are found within this word search. The names are written across, down, and diagonally.

```
C O N N N E T I C U T V E R M O N T A G L K
E U R O P E S W A S H I N G T O N E M E O E
A R I Z O N A H C O L O R A D O E W I O U N
P E N N S Y L V A N I A T O N S B F N R I T
N R M E X I C O N W I N A R S I R L N G S U
S O U T H D A K O T A N E E X O A O E I I C
M A R Y L A N D N P I I N W O W S R S A A K
O R U T A H R A N L G N I E J A K I O B N Y
N K A O H O K W O A E R E D V E A D T S A T
E T L S U C S R A T C H I L E A R A A C W S
W E A A J O A M I S S O U R I R D S J F E L
Y X S N H C L R M I C H I G A N N A E M S R
O A K A H O W Y O M I N G V T A D A D Y T H
R S A T M A M E H L O O K I K L L D I E V O
K N U P E R U A I O I M O R I A T A N L I D
N O R T H D A K O T A N A G N B N I D A R E
S R C A L I F O R N I A A I D A A S I N G I
N E W H A M P S H I R E B N I M O E A D I S
O G M I S S I S S I P P I I A A L M N S N L
M O N T A N A T O Y D E L A W A R E A T I A
A N E W M E X I C O E W I S C O N S I N A N
M A S S A C H U S E T T S I L L I N O I S D
```

Alabama
Alaska
Arizona
Arkansas
California
Colorado
Connecticut
Delaware
Florida
Georgia
Hawaii
Idaho
Illinois
Indiana
Iowa
Kansas
Kentucky
Louisiana
Maine
Maryland
Massachusetts
Michigan
Minnesota
Mississippi
Missouri
Montana
Nebraska
Nevada
New Hampshire
New Jersey
New Mexico
New York
North Carolina
North Dakota
Ohio
Oklahoma
Oregon
Pennsylvania
Rhode Island
South Carolina
South Dakota
Tennessee
Texas
Utah
Vermont
Virginia
Washington
West Virginia
Wisconsin
Wyoming

FALL

Across

1. The season after summer
4. How do you _____
6. Opposite of woman
7. Used to drink an ice-cream soda
9. Animal doctors
11. Time before noon
12. Finish
14. A home for birds
16. ___ what
19. Fall sport

Down

2. Another name for fall
3. These fall in fall in the North
4. Fathers
5. Not off
8. She _____ away
10. Short for touchdown
13. The night air turns _____ in fall
15. A, __, __, __, U
17. The Wizard ___ Oz
18. Another word for Dad

SPORTS

Across

2. You need it for one kind of skating
4. Letters that sound like empty
6. Fisherman uses one
8. Not happy
9. You knock them down in bowling
10. David's nickname
11. All right
12. Used to shoot arrows
14. Home _____
15. To use your eyes
16. Game played with clubs
19. Opposite of isn't
21. Boxers wear them
23. You kick a ball with this part of your shoe

Down

1. Opposite of yes
3. Baseball player wears one on his head
4. Catcher or goalie wears one
5. Abbreviation for touchdown
6. What a jockey is
7. Way to get in the water
8. You can ski after it _____
12. It's used in many games
13. They are used in tennis
17. Letters that say "Oh, gee"
18. Opposite of against
19. Throw ___ to me
20. Rhymes with go
22. Short for Emily

MAKE A WORD

1. If students begin to finish an assignment early, the teacher can put one of the following on the board for the students to work.

2. The students are to use the letters to make as many different words as they can of three or more letters. The letters may be used only once in each word (there are over thirty possible words that may be made).

3. The student with the longest word or the most words may read his list to the class and be the first one in line when class is dismissed.

Examples:

S	O	N
T	I	E
R	C	U

S	E	D
M	I	T
C	S	O

A	L	R
E	E	T
C	O	N

P	I	R
L	A	K
S	G	N

N	E	D
R	A	R
W	G	I

L	U	A
R	S	O
V	E	M

INSTANT SUCCESS ©

Break Activities

This unit may be used during breaks such as before lunch, recess, or dismissal, between subjects, or when students become restless. This unit may also be used in conjunction with the Discipline unit.

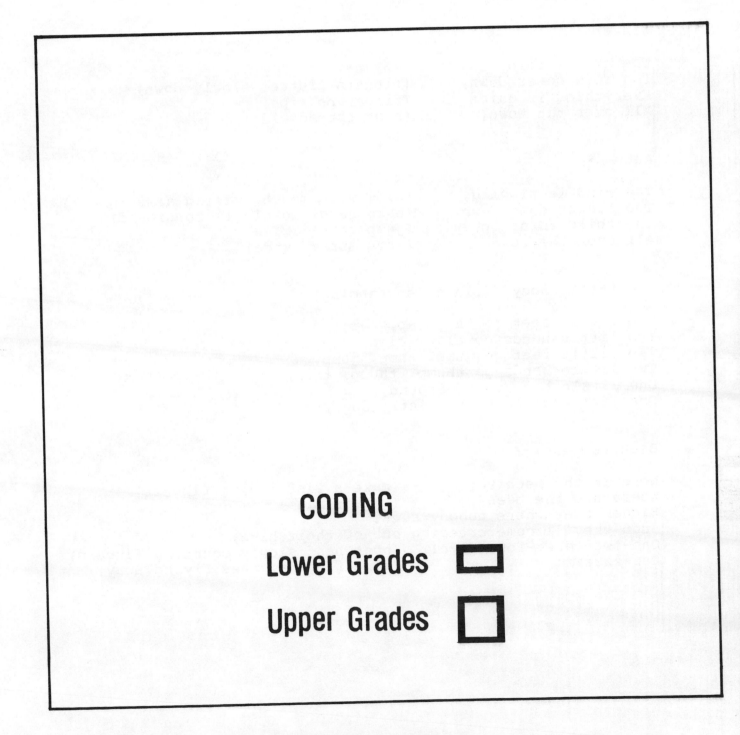

CODING

Lower Grades ▭

Upper Grades ▭

Spring

The sun is warm,	(make a big sun with arms)
The rain came down,	(fingers flutter to floor)
The flowers are growing	(stoop, raise fingers slowly above head)
All over the town.	(arms spread wide)

Winter

The air is cold,	(shiver)
The snow comes down,	(fingers flutter slowly down)
Everything is quiet	(finger on lips)
All over the town.	(arms spread wide)

Autumn

The wind is blowing,	(blow with mouth, waving arms in air)
The leaves come down,	(make hands go slowly to ground)
The children are playing	(jump rope)
All over the town.	(arms spread wide)

One Little Body (class is standing)

Two little feet go tap, tap, tap,
Two little hands go clap, clap, clap,
Two little feet go jump, jump, jump,
Two little hands go thump, thump, thump,
One little body turns around,
One little child sits quietly down.

Beehive

Here is the beehive.	(make a fist hiding fingers)
Where are the bees?	(rotate fist)
Hidden away where nobody sees.	
Soon they'll come creeping out of their hive,	
One-two-three-four-five!	(open hand slowly counting fingers)
Buzzzzzzzz!	(move fingers, bees flying away)

INSTANT SUCCESS ©

Birds

Two little blackbirds sitting on a hill.   (hold up pointer fin-
                                              gers)
One named Jack, one named Jill.   (move one finger at a time)
Fly away Jack, fly away Jill.   (put each finger behind body)
Come back Jack, come back Jill.   (return each finger to front
                                      of body)

The Orange Balloon

I have a small, orange, round balloon. (put finger and thumb
                                          together in a circle)
I blow it up.   (blow, use two hands, make the balloon bigger)
And I blow it up.   (make it bigger)
Now I have a big, orange, round balloon. (the same)
I blow it up some more.   (make it bigger)
And I blow it up some more.   (make it bigger)
And I blow it up some more.   (make it bigger)
Now I have a big, big, orange round--POP! (big clap)
Oh, dear.   (sigh)
Now I have a small, orange, flat balloon. (hand palm up)

Little Rabbit

In a cabin in the woods   (make roof with two hands arched)
Little man by the window stood   (stand up straight)
Little rabbit hopping by (hold up fist with two fingers, move
                            hand up and down)
Knocking at my door.   (make fist and knock)
"Help me, help me, help me," he said   (pantomime words express-
                                          ing fear)
"Before the hunter shoots me dead."   (hold rifle and shoot)
"Little rabbit come inside,   (open door and signal to come in)
Safely here you can hide."   (cradle in arms)

Little Boy in Bed

This little boy is going to bed,   (yawn)
And on this pillow he lays his head.   (put hands together,
                                           put head on top)
He takes the covers and wraps up tight,   (pull up covers and
                                           snuggle)
And this is the way he sleeps all night. (put head on pillow
                                           and close eyes)
When morning comes, he opens his eyes,   (open up eyes)
And back with a jerk the covers fly.   (throw off covers)
He jumps out of bed and puts on his clothes, (jump and dress)
And off to school and play he goes.   (skip)

Lion Hunt

Teacher asks class, "Who wants to go on a lion hunt?" The students respond, "I do." The class acts out each verse with the teacher while the teacher does all the talking.

1. Wake up everyone and let's get going on a lion hunt. Let's dress quickly so we can go on a lion hunt. Let's eat a good breakfast before we go on a lion hunt. Let's wash up and brush our teeth before we go on a lion hunt. Let's get on our heavy coat and hat and get our gun to go on a lion hunt. Close the door and let's go.

The teacher and the students now begin a rhythm of slapping hands against knees as if walking.

2. There's a river. Can't go round it, can't go over it, must go through it. O.K. Let's go. (pretend you are swimming)

Pretend to be walking again.

3. There's a big field. Can't go round it, can't go over it, must go through it. O.K. Let's go. (rub hands back and forth together)

Walking again.

4. There's a swamp. Can't go under it, can't go over it, must go through it. O.K. Let's go. (cup hands palms down, raise cupped hands alternately up and down making suction noise with mouth)

Walking.

5. There's a forest. Can't go under it, can't go over it, must climb through it. O.K. Let's go. (pretend to climb rope)

Walking.

6. There's a mountain. Can't go round it, must go over it. O.K. Let's go. (hit hands on knees the same as walking only slower to show climbing) We're on top so let's run down the other side. (hit hands on knees rapidly)

7. There's the lion's cave. Let's tiptoe in. (tiptoe with fingers) Take your rifle. I see a lion. SHOOT! You missed. Run fast out of the cave. Up the mountain. (repeating each motion). Through the forest. Through the swamp. Through the big field. Through the river. Home at last. (close the door and sigh)

MIXED-UP SENTENCES

The teacher makes a statement to the class that is nonsense.
The class is to determine what is mixed up about the statement.

Examples:

When I am hungry, I go to the North Pole to make a sandwich.

When it's dark, I turn on the chair.

I ride to school on my bed.

Jack be nimble, Jack be quick,
Jack jump over the handle stick.

Jack and Bill went up the hill
To fetch a pail of water.

Hickory, dickory, dock!
The house ran up the clock.

Little Boy Blue, come blow your thorn.
The sheep's in the meadow, the cow's in the corn.

Simple Simon met a pieman
Going to the chair.

Mary had a little lamb,
Its fleece was bright as snow.

Three blind rice! See how they run!
They all ran after the farmer's wife.

Humpty Dumpty sat on a wall,
Humpty Bumpty had a great fall!

Twinkle, twinkle little car,
How I wonder what you are!

One, two, buckle my shoe;
Three, four, shut the floor.

Pat-a-cake, pat-a-cake, baker's man.
Bake me a lake as fast as you can.

Baa, baa, black sheep, have you any wool?
Yes, sir; yes sir...free bags full.

RHYMING AND OPPOSITES

The teacher reads the phrase or word and asks a student to respond with an opposite or rhyming word.

Rhymes

A color, rhymes with bed	(red)
A place, rhymes with mouse	(house)
An animal, rhymes with coat	(goat)
A food, rhymes with make	(cake)
A color, rhymes with crown	(brown)
Something you ride in, rhymes with far	(car)
A toy, rhymes with call	(ball)
An animal, rhymes with mitten	(kitten)
A person, rhymes with other	(mother)
Something you ride in, rhymes with rain	(train)
An animal, rhymes with house	(mouse)
A color, rhymes with fellow	(yellow)
Something to wear, rhymes with lock	(sock)
A number, rhymes with dive	(five)
An animal, rhymes with pear	(bear)
A color, rhymes with kite	(white)
Furniture, rhymes with cable	(table)
A flower, rhymes with nose	(rose)
Something you ride in, rhymes with coat	(boat)
Furniture, rhymes with red	(bed)

Opposites

in	(out)
big	(little)
night	(day)
open	(shut)
sad	(happy)
go	(stop)
wrong	(right)
dirty	(clean)
poor	(rich)
soft	(hard)
slow	(fast)
ask	(answer)
broken	(fix)
cold	(hot)
asleep	(awake)
carry	(drop)
begin	(end)
start	(finish)
dark	(light)
full	(empty)
large	(small)

INSTANT SUCCESS ©

CLUES

The teacher reads, "It is used for" and describes an object. A student is asked to guess the name.

Examples:

It is used for:
    cooking dinner   (stove)
    wearing on your head   (hat)
    lighting a fire   (match)
    telling time   (clock)
    riding to school   (bicycle)
    cleaning your teeth   (toothbrush)
    cutting meat   (knife)
    keeping food cold   (refrigerator)
    taking pictures   (camera)
    flying   (airplane)
    calling people to talk   (telephone)
    light   (lamp)
    holding things together   (glue)
    eating on   (table)

HOW WERE THEY TRAVELING

The teacher says, "I'm going to read you a sentence. I will then call on one of you to guess how the person in the sentence is traveling. Try to guess if it is by helicopter, train, boat, bus, plane, or car."

Examples:

As Pam was riding with her husband on the freeway, she said, "I wish you would keep your speed down."   (car)

Ken was almost asleep when he heard the porter shout, "Last call for dinner, dining car to the rear."   (train)

"I thought we would never get into New York," said Gary. "We stopped at so many places along the road to let passengers off and to take on others."   (bus)

Paul said to his daughter beside him, "This thing shakes more, makes more noise, and goes slower than a plane does; but, we can look down on the tall buildings of the city."   (helicopter)

It was a wonderful trip," said Kathy, "but the sea was rough at times. Some people got seasick, but I didn't." (boat)

"In coming from Washington, D.C. to New York, we landed in Philadelphia," said David.   (plane)

INSTANT SUCCESS ©

OCCUPATIONS

The teacher makes a statement and a student is asked to guess the occupation.

Examples:

I style hair to make people look more attractive. (hair dresser)

I usually work downtown. I help the businessmen by making their shoes look nice and shiny. (shoeshine person)

I'm a very important person. I tell the sailors what jobs they are to do. I have to be sure the ship is sailing properly. (ship's captain)

Children are always glad when I come to their house. I fix a certain item. When I am finished, they can watch their favorite program. (television repairman)

My job begins very early in the morning. I take a black and white item to people's homes. When they wake up, they may read about the news around the world. (paper boy)

Working on cars is my job. I know just how to get them running again. (mechanic)

I wear a neat uniform. When I work, I always carry a glove and bat. I love to run the bases. (baseball player)

I take your food order. I bring your water. I serve your food. Then I bring your check. (waiter)

I sit at a desk all day. I answer the telephone. I type letters. (secretary)

I work outdoors most of the time. I plow, plant seeds, and harvest my crops. (farmer)

I work on my toes. I wear a special kind of shoe. I move gracefully with the music. (ballet dancer)

I work on electric cords and wires. If your house needs electricity, please call on me. (electrician)

KNOCKING PATTERNS

1. The teacher knocks on a desk three or more times with a pause between one or more of the knocks.

2. The teacher asks a student if he can repeat the knocking pattern.

3. The student responds by attempting to repeat the pattern on his desk.

4. If incorrect, the teacher repeats the pattern and calls on another student.

5. If correct, the teacher changes the pattern and begins over again.

INSTANT SUCCESS ©

TEAM DIRECTIONS

1. The teacher divides the class into two teams.

2. The teacher gives a series of three directions to a student she selects from each team. The number and degree of difficulty may be increased with grade level.

3. Each student who follows the series of directions accurately scores one point for his team.

Examples:

Write your name on the chalkboard.
Put the chalk on the back table.
Pick up a book on the back table and put it on the teacher's desk.

Mirror Exercises

During all pantomime activities the students are to stand in an empty space. There is to be no talking while the activities are taking place.

1. The teacher initiates a movement such as raising her right arm and the class copies the movement as if they are her mirror image. Additional arm movements could be throwing a ball, swimming, climbing, etc. All movements are done in slow motion.

2. Everyone needs a partner for this activity. A is looking into the mirror. B is the mirror and makes whatever movements A makes. Only arms should be used. Again, all movements are done in slow motion. The teacher asks the students to reverse roles after an appropriate time.

Walk to Words

1. The teacher asks the students to begin walking about the room. Each student should walk in spaces where no one else is walking. On command, the students should follow the teacher's directions which might tell the students to walk quickly, slowly, backward, forward, on toes, on heels, in the opposite direction, etc.

2. The teacher calls out a number from 2 to 6. The students get together with one another to form groups. The number of students in each group should be the same as the number called out by the teacher.

3. The teacher asks the students to pretend they are walking along a narrow ledge, in the wind, in the rain, in sticky mud, on hot sand, in a crowded street, in a dark alley, with a sore foot, etc.

4. The teacher asks the students to pretend to be the following circus performers: walk on a high wire, a lion tamer in a cage with several lions, a clown, a strong man, a dancing elephant, etc.

5. The teacher asks the students to walk as if they are angry, mean, sleepy, strong, weak, suspicious, lazy, excited, sad, etc.

INSTANT SUCCESS ©

Sensory Expressions

1. The teacher asks the students to pretend they are thirsty, cold, hot, or eating the following: peanut butter, corn on the cob, tough steak, a lemon, cotton candy, ice cream, etc.

2. The teacher asks the students to pretend they are smelling flowers, gasoline, a cigar, a skunk, a turkey on Thanksgiving, etc.

3. The teacher asks the students to pretend they are hearing rock and roll music, an emergency siren, an alarm clock ringing, holiday music, being reminded to do chores, etc.

4. The teacher asks the students to pretend they are feeling velvet, a man's beard, a raw egg, a hot stove, snow, etc.

Movement Experiences

1. The teacher asks the students to pretend they are:

   a cat with a sore paw
   a balloon being stretched, blown up, caught in the wind, bumped, and popped
   trying to sneak up creaky stairs
   popcorn popping
   a flower opening up and then wilting
   a light bulb winding into a socket and turning on brightly
   a jet plane taking off
   a washing machine washing clothes
   a steam shovel digging a hole

2. The teacher asks the students to pretend they are puppets. There are strings on their wrists, legs, and head. The teacher gives directions as to which string she will pull, and the students will respond with jerky motions. Finally all the strings are let go at the same time.

3. The teacher asks the students to pretend they are walking under water (slow motion), then swimming with the fish, seeing a shark, and being saved by a whale.

4. The teacher asks the students to pretend they are walking through streams, over rocks, around trees, and climbing up to the top of a mountain.

5. The teacher asks the students to pretend they are exploring a cave. It is dark and cold, a mouse runs by and bats fly by. A roar is heard, the students run and become lost. They see daylight, a river flows nearby, so they swim to safety.

PANTOMIME CARDS

1. A student is chosen to pick a card from an envelope and pretends to use the item named on the card. The first student who correctly guesses the item becomes the next student to pick a card.

2. As an alternative, the student picking the card can pretend to work at an occupation.

3. As another alternative, the student picking the card can pretend to be an animal.

Examples:

Items: newspaper, vacuum cleaner, lawnmower, umbrella, shoe polish, glue, candle, cough drop, toothbrush, football, bicycle, typewriter.

Occupations: policeman, baseball player, golfer, tennis player, fisherman, secretary, telephone operator, barber, carpenter, teacher, cook, farmer, King/Queen.

Animals: dog, cat, lion, horse, ant, bear, elephant, skunk, mosquito, bird, snake, chicken, monkey.

INSTANT SUCCESS ©

NUMBERS HIGHER AND LOWER

1. The teacher writes a two-digit number on a piece of paper.

2. A student is asked to guess the number. If the guess is higher than the teacher's number, it is written high on the chalkboard. If lower, it is written low on the chalkboard.

3. Other students are asked to guess the number. Their guesses are placed on the chalkboard in a column either higher or lower than the teacher's number and in proper sequence with the other numbers.

4. If a guess is made that is higher or lower than the range of guesses already recorded, it is called a wasted guess and is written outside the column of numbers (see example below).

Example:

(1st guess)	70		
(5th guess)	50	90	(7th guess - a wasted guess)
(8th guess)	(48)		(the teacher's number)
(6th guess)	42		
(3rd guess)	37	16	(4th guess - a wasted guess)
(2nd guess)	22		

MENTAL MATH

1. The teacher reads the math combination and the students do all the computations mentally.

2. The teacher calls on a student for the correct answer.

Examples:

```
2 + 3 - 3 =        (2)
3 + 7 - 1 =        (9)
4 X 2 + 2 =       (10)
7 X 2 + 3 =       (17)
4 X 5 + 5 =       (25)
3 X 4 + 2 =       (14)
9 X 3 - 2 =       (25)
15 - 6 + 8 =      (17)
10 - 7 + 6 =       (9)
1 + 4 - 2 + 5 = (8)
```

```
2 X 8 ÷ 4 + 3 - 2 =     (5)
5 X 8 ÷ 4 - 6 + 5 =     (9)
9 ÷ 3 X 5 - 9 + 2 =     (8)
2 X 9 ÷ 3 + 9 - 3 =    (12)
7 X 6 ÷ 2 + 4 - 5 =    (20)
5 X 6 ÷ 3 + 9 + 1 =    (20)
8 ÷ 2 X 8 - 4 + 3 =    (31)
24 ÷ 6 X 7 - 3     =   (25)
10 X 6 ÷ 3 + 13    =   (33)
10 X 10 ÷ 2 - 3    =   (47)
```

INSTANT SUCCESS ©

MIXED MATH

1. The teacher reads a series of statements involving different units of measurement.

2. The students write the answer on a piece of paper and raise their hands when they have calculated the answer.

3. The teacher calls on one of the students to give his answer.

Examples:

Write the number of days in a week	7
Add the number of wheels on a car (4)	11
Add the inches in a foot (12)	23
Add the number of toes on your left foot (5)	28
Add the number of dimes in a dollar (10)	38
Add the number of minutes in an hour (60)	98
Add the number of legs on a bird (2)	100

Write the number of pennies in a nickel	5
Multiply by the number of nickels in a quarter (5)	25
Add the number of players on a baseball team (9)	34
Add the number of pints in a quart (2)	36
Divide by the number of inches in a foot (12)	3

Write the number of pounds in half a ton	1000
Multiply by the number of feet on a dog (4)	4000
Divide by the number of nickels in a dollar (20)	200
Subtract the number of inches in a yard (36)	164
Divide by the number of quarts in a gallon (4)	41

Write the number of pennies in a dollar	100
Multiply by the number of thirds in a circle (3)	300
Divide by the number of inches in a foot of yarn (12)	25
Subtract the number of nickles in a quarter (5)	20

Write the number of days in September	30
Multiply by the number of ten's in 50 (5)	150
Divide by the number of eyes a cat has (2)	75
Subtract the number of days in a week (7)	68
Add the number of leaves on a four-leaf clover (4)	72

BUZZ

1. The teacher asks the students to stand by their desks.

2. They are to start counting down the classroom rows beginning with 1, and every time a 5 or a multiple of 5 is mentioned, "Buzz" is said instead of the number.

3. If any student says a 5 or multiple of 5, he is out of the game and sits down in his chair.

Example:

1, 2, 3, 4, "Buzz," 6, 7, 8, 9, "Buzz," 11, 12, 13, 14, "Buzz," 16, 17, 18, 19, "Buzz," 21, etc.

4. The game continues, starting with 1 again.

5. It may be played with a 3 or a multiple of 3.

Example:

1, 2, "Buzz," 4, 5, "Buzz," 7, 8, "Buzz," 10, 11, "Buzz," "Buzz," 14, "Buzz," 16, 17, "Buzz," 19, 20, "Buzz," 22, "Buzz," "Buzz," 25, etc.

6. It may be played with a 7 or a multiple of 7.

Example:

1, 2, 3, 4, 5, 6, "Buzz," 8, 9, 10, 11, 12, 13, "Buzz," 15, 16, "Buzz," 18, 19, 20, "Buzz," 22, etc.

7. To make the game difficult, it may be played with both 3's and 7's and their multiples.

Example:

1, 2, "Buzz," 4, 5, "Buzz," "Buzz," 8, "Buzz," 10, 11, "Buzz," "Buzz," "Buzz," "Buzz," 16, "Buzz," "Buzz," 19, 20, "Buzz," 22, "Buzz," "Buzz," 25, 26, "Buzz," "Buzz," 29 "Buzz," 31, etc.

8. The object is to see how far the students can count without missing a "Buzz."

INSTANT SUCCESS ©

DISCIPLINE

"I can't teach when I can't control the class!" Not all classes
require the substitute to control class behavior. Occasionally
there are no disruptive situations. When disruptive situations
do occur, it is important to determine the type of disruption,
get the attention of the class, implement discipline strategies
to correct the disruptive situation, and plan for free time as a
reward.

I. Identifying the type of disruption requiring discipline:

A. Behavior disruption is noise created by either one
   student, a small group of students, or the entire
   class that interferes with the learning atmosphere of
   the classroom.

B. Movement disruption is sharpening pencils, abusing
   restroom privileges, getting drinks, getting paper, or
   other activities that interfere with the learning
   atmosphere of the classroom.

II. Techniques for obtaining the attention of the class:

A. Primary grades: Write directions on the board, flick
   the lights, announce "Heads down," look sternly at
   the class, start rhythm activity with clapping, talk
   to class with a firm voice, approach the disruptive
   student and privately discuss the rules with him,
   positive reinforcement for those listening (directions
   for any activity may be sung for kindergarten students).

B. Upper grades: Write directions on the board, look
   sternly at the class, drop a book sharply on a desk,
   talk to the class with a firm voice, approach the
   disruptive student and privately discuss the rules
   with him, positive reinforcement for those listening.

III. Discipline strategies:

A. List of good workers: Make a list of the students displaying GOOD work habits, overlooking those with disruptive behaviors. Have a reliable student write the names for the list as the teacher points to those in the class who are working quietly. Only the teacher can determine what students' names go on the list. (K-2, the teacher writes the list on the board.) Names may be taken off the list for disruptive behavior. Resumption of good behavior can restore a student's name to the list. The list may be left for the classroom teacher or as a method for dismissing students from the room.

B. Earning free time:

1. Once a disturbance has occurred, the teacher states, "I notice the class enjoys free time. I have to follow the lesson plans, but you will be able to earn free time at the end of the class period by following the GROUND RULES."

2. The teacher then says, "There are only two GROUND RULES. The first rule is: if you have anything to say, raise your hand. There will be no talking without permission. The second rule is: if you wish to leave your desk, raise your hand. NO ONE is to disturb the learning atmosphere of others."

3. Divide the class into equal groups. List the groups on the board. The groups may consist of rows (1, 2, 3, 4, etc.), clusters of students identified by a student's name (John, Mary, etc.), or divided into two groups (boys, girls).

4. Explain that if one person from a specific group forgets the rules, the teacher places a mark (called a reminder mark) under their group on the board. Each group works for free time independent of the other groups. They are allowed three reminder marks (usually adequate for an hour's time).

5. Those who fail to earn free time because their group has four or more reminder marks will continue working on their assignment or have an additional assignment while the others are having free time.

INSTANT SUCCESS ©

6. Do not discuss it any further. The entire class will decide the free time activity ONLY at the end of the class period (eight minutes before class is over). Ask if there are any questions and begin. This explanation should take only a few minutes. Be strict at first and more generous to those who have difficulty succeeding.

7. If a group has a disruptive student, he can be placed in his own group (separate from the others) taking his marks with him.

8. If any group has more than three reminder marks, they may earn the removal of reminder marks by exhibiting good behavior. For every five minutes of good behavior, according to the ground rules, a reminder mark will be erased. This is to be used sparingly as the students will take advantage of the situation.

9. Once free time has come, (eight minutes before class ends), those who earned it will vote on what they wish to do during this time. Suggestions for free time are made by the teacher and the class. The activities in the Rapport Builders and Break Activities units are also possibilities for use during free time.

10. Reminder: If the action of a student is not included in the ground rules, it must be dealt with differently and not interfere with earning free time.

11. This strategy should be used for no more than an hour at a time. It may be used at other times during the day, but should be alternated with other discipline strategies.

C. Positive reinforcement: The teacher tells the class, "I enjoy working with a class whose behavior is this great. You are all very special." For a specific student, "Thank you, Jim, for working so hard" (said only to him). For primary grades, the teacher tells the class that those working quietly will feel a pat on their head. Then touch each student on the head who is working quietly.

D. Time out: If one student persists in being a problem in the class, he needs to be placed in an area away from the majority of the students for as much time as he feels is necessary. He may return to his place when he feels he can behave in an acceptable manner. Otherwise, he will sit where the teacher chooses to place him.

E. Working quietly: Every five minutes that one or more groups work quietly, the teacher records points for those groups (1 through 4 or whatever number of groups are established). The groups with the most points are dismissed first for recess, end of day, etc. If all groups receive equal points, they are dismissed together.

F. Agreement: Special privileges are privately discussed between a student and the teacher for a desired behavior. Good behavior is reinforced by trading points for privileges. Every five minutes of good behavior is equal to one point. Five points provides five minutes of QUIET free time to be used for the bathroom, drinks, helper, errands, etc.

G. Chronically disruptive student: He may earn free time for the entire class. If he agrees, a star is put on the board for every five minutes of his good behavior. A specific number of stars earns eight minutes free time for the entire class (8 stars per 52 minutes is adequate).

H. Principal's office: If the student becomes too difficult for class control, and all else fails, the student is sent to the principal's office accompanied by another student. If the student is not sent, a note is taken to the office requesting the principal to visit your room immediately.

INSTANT SUCCESS ©

IV. Activities for eight-minute free time:

All activities are listed on the board and then decided on by class voting. All students have the choice to continue working on their assignment during free time. Those who have not earned free time are REQUIRED to work on their assignment.

A. Primary: Any suggestions from the class, games familiar to the teacher with the rules thoroughly discussed, charades, story, quiet talking time, five minutes added to the supervised recess period, activities in Rapport Builders and Break Activities.

B. Upper: Any suggestions from the class, games familiar to the teacher with the rules thoroughly discussed, charades, a good short story, quiet talking time, activities in Rapport Builders and Break Activities.

Graphic Riddles (page 21)

1. sit down
2. I understand
3. red overcoat
4. double time
5. cross roads
6. four-wheel drive
7. downtown
8. six feet under ground
9. good afternoon
10. split personality
11. Seven Seas
12. one after another
13. head over heels
14. different strokes
15. tricycle
16. just between you and me
17. age before beauty
18. generation gap
19. backward glance
20. broken engagement
21. 1 if by land, 2 if by sea
22. getting it altogether
23. eggs over easy
24. paradise
25. mixed-up kid
26. double trouble
27. scrambled eggs
28. three-ring circus

Scrambled Eggs (page 48)

1. robin
2. wren
3. duck
4. snake
5. swan
6. stork
7. turkey
8. parakeet
9. bluejay
10. seagull
11. eagle
12. ostrich
13. goose
14. dove
15. pelican
16. chicken
17. turtle
18. canary
19. lizard
20. alligator

Spellers (page 49)

1. asinine
2. liquefy
3. fantasies
4. tracheotomy
5. conscientious
6. impostor
7. moccasin
8. accommodate
9. consensus
10. hallucinate
11. mayonaise
12. inoculate
13. renaissance
14. photography
15. resuscitate
16. appropriate

Decode the Riddle (page 74 and page 75)

What always follows a lion everywhere?   his tail
What happens at the end of a dry spell?   rain

Seasonal Sports Activities (page 77)

Fall: football, hopscotch, jump rope, jacks, soccer, marbles
Winter: hockey, skiing, sledding, basketball, gymnastics, ice
        skating
Spring: tennis, kites, hiking, track, baseball, bicycling
Summer: camping, fishing, golf, boating, surfing, swimming

INSTANT SUCCESS ©

CROSSWORD MATH

CROSSWORD MATH

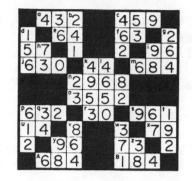

SCRAMBLED MONTHS

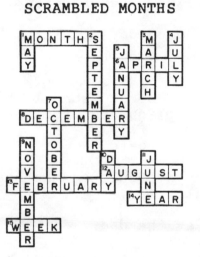

FALL

SPORTS

PROCEDURES

Substitute's Responsibility

1. To the School: There should be no criticism of any teacher or any student. Such criticism is not professional and will not serve the best interest of the students. Do not release a student from school without the knowledge of the office.

2. To the Regular Teacher: Make every effort to carry on the program of the regular teacher and not disrupt the student's learning process. A note should be left to cover the day's events. See sample on page 111 (courtesy of Scottsdale Schools).

3. To the Students: Follow their routine as nearly as possible and provide a good experience for them.

4. To Herself: Have a good day!

Management

1. The substitute should be at school thirty minutes early. Look over the lesson plans and prepare for the day.

2. Write your name on the board.

3. Write the teacher's schedule on the board including recess, lunch, and dismissal times.

4. Greet the students at the door.

5. Have a sense of humor. A smile works wonders!

First Ten Minutes

1. Introduce yourself.

2. Tell a little about yourself (where you're from, your hobbies, about your family).

3. If you need information about something in the room, phrase your questions so the students will raise their hands or so only one student will answer.

4. Read to the class the part of the teacher's note about class control (if appropriate) and the assignment for the first part of the morning. As the day progresses, continue to read her instructions.

INSTANT SUCCESS ©

5. If students are well behaved, tell them. If discipline is necessary, tell those who are behaving inappropriately that their actions are unacceptable. Then explain what is acceptable. "You may not disturb the learning atmosphere of others in the class and you are to do the work your teacher assigned for you."

6. If necessary, a discipline technique may be implemented (refer to page 101).

7. Continue by telling the class, "Before we start our day, let's do some other things first." Tell a few jokes, riddles, etc. from Rapport Builders and then tell them that it is now necessary to follow the lesson plans, but that you will do more at the end of the class period. Be sure you follow through with what you say!

Routine

1. Keep students busy! It will decrease discipline problems. Have plenty of activities planned just in case you need them.

2. Find things in the room to make complimentary remarks about. Be positive about being in the room with the class. Make sure every student has some success or praise each day you're there. The students are pleased when you remember their names.

3. Be firm. Be sure of yourself. Uncertainty invites trouble. Give the student a choice when disciplining (the student's own suggestions or your options). If he continues to be a discipline problem, follow through with the consequence. Don't give many second chances, sometimes the first warning is enough. Make every effort to keep your cool. Most important is to be honest with them.

4. It is advisable to maintain eye contact with the class throughout the day.

5. Start relaxing, even laugh when appropriate. Be enthusiastic.

End of day

1. Go over your note to the teacher with the students so there will be no misunderstandings.

2. When dismissing students, stand by the door to prevent thirty students from running through the door all at once.

Bad Memories: I've had nine years of substituting success with only a few instances of "bad days." The following are some of the things I've had go wrong. Sharing them may help you realize that you may also have a "bad day." It's part of the game!

1. 8th grade: A student threw an eraser and I immediately started using a discipline technique (page 101). The class responded well; then I followed the lesson plans. My good friend's daughter was in class. She went to a special class and left during the chaos. She returned during the last five minutes which they earned as free time. They were visiting with each other and it appeared as though the class was in disorder. I've never mentioned this incident to my friend. I was too embarrassed.

2. 8th grade: While I was taking attendance, someone removed the film strip projector's lens. A good portion of class time was taken up with negotiating it back, including the principal visiting our class.

3. 7th grade: I did not know that a boy was on the verge of being expelled from school. The day I substituted, he was holding a tape recorder by the cord and swinging it around. He was pushing several girls around and finally hit another student. He was expelled that day. I felt responsible.

4. 6th grade: The entire class coughed in unison at 2:15 and again at 2:25. I then said, "That's enough," and laughed. "At the count of three I want everyone to get it out of their system and cough together. Those coughing later on will stay in at recess since they're too sick to go out. 1-2-3." They all "screamed" and we were in a room shared with four other teachers. All became instantly aware of my "terrific" solution.

5. 6th grade: The film projector broke just before showing two long films that were scheduled. Also, there was no answer key available for the class to correct a very difficult science test. Fortunately, it was my favorite class and they were very understanding. I can't remember what we did instead (amnesia). It was too painful to remember.

6. 2nd grade: I came in to substitute for the last one and one-half hours of class time. It was a team teaching situation and the other teacher was also a substitute. We had students under chairs, on desk tops, and pushing and pulling. There was absolute chaos during the film. We stopped the film and quickly gave the students seatwork for the rest of the hour. What a way to earn a half day's pay! (Half days are usually my easiest jobs.)

7. Kindergarten: It was the last day of school before the Christmas holidays. The teacher had not been in class for a week and three substitutes were there before me. There were no lesson plans. I had to frantically finish getting things off the Christmas tree and sorted for the students to take home. I had to gather materials from who knows where for an art activity. What a day to remember!

8. All grades: There have been innumerable incidents when I have asked a question of the class and everyone answers loudly at once, or the answers all differ and the students begin arguing. Another time no one understood the assignment and they all swarmed on me at once. There are the times with flying airplanes and spit wads which I never saw until I heard the students laughing about them when they left the room. Also, I'll never forget the day I misread the lesson plans for first grade and dismissed the students at clean-up time. I then had to round them up when I realized no other class had left. I reread the lesson plans and found I had dismissed them twenty minutes early.

9. Remember that these kinds of things can happen to anyone! Hopefully your day will be a good one. There is nothing in my experience that can feel so good as to know the students have enjoyed their day.

Substitute teachers must be the most flexible teachers of all. They must establish a rapport which gives them a climate in which to teach. Substitutes are NOT baby sitters. They are teachers.

SUBSTITUTE
TEACHER'S
REPORT

SCOTTSDALE PUBLIC SCHOOLS   DATE:_____

SUBSTITUTE TEACHER'S REPORT TO REGULAR TEACHER - PLEASE COMPLETE THIS FORM,
AND TURN IT IN WITH YOUR KEYS AND FOLDER, AT THE CLOSE OF THE SCHOOL DAY.

Substitute Teacher_____ Dates Worked_____

Regular Teacher_____

Please report briefly on the following:

1. Work completed by the class in all subject areas:_____
_____
_____
_____
_____
_____

2. Assignments given for the following day: (Not compulsory)_____

3. General Discipline Report: (List here any pupils who were especially
   helpful, or any pupils whose lack of cooperation should be called to
   the attention of the regular teacher.)_____
_____
_____
_____

4. School Business: (List here any information about announcements made,
   monies collected, etc., which would be of interest to the regular
   teacher.)_____
_____
_____

5. Remarks: